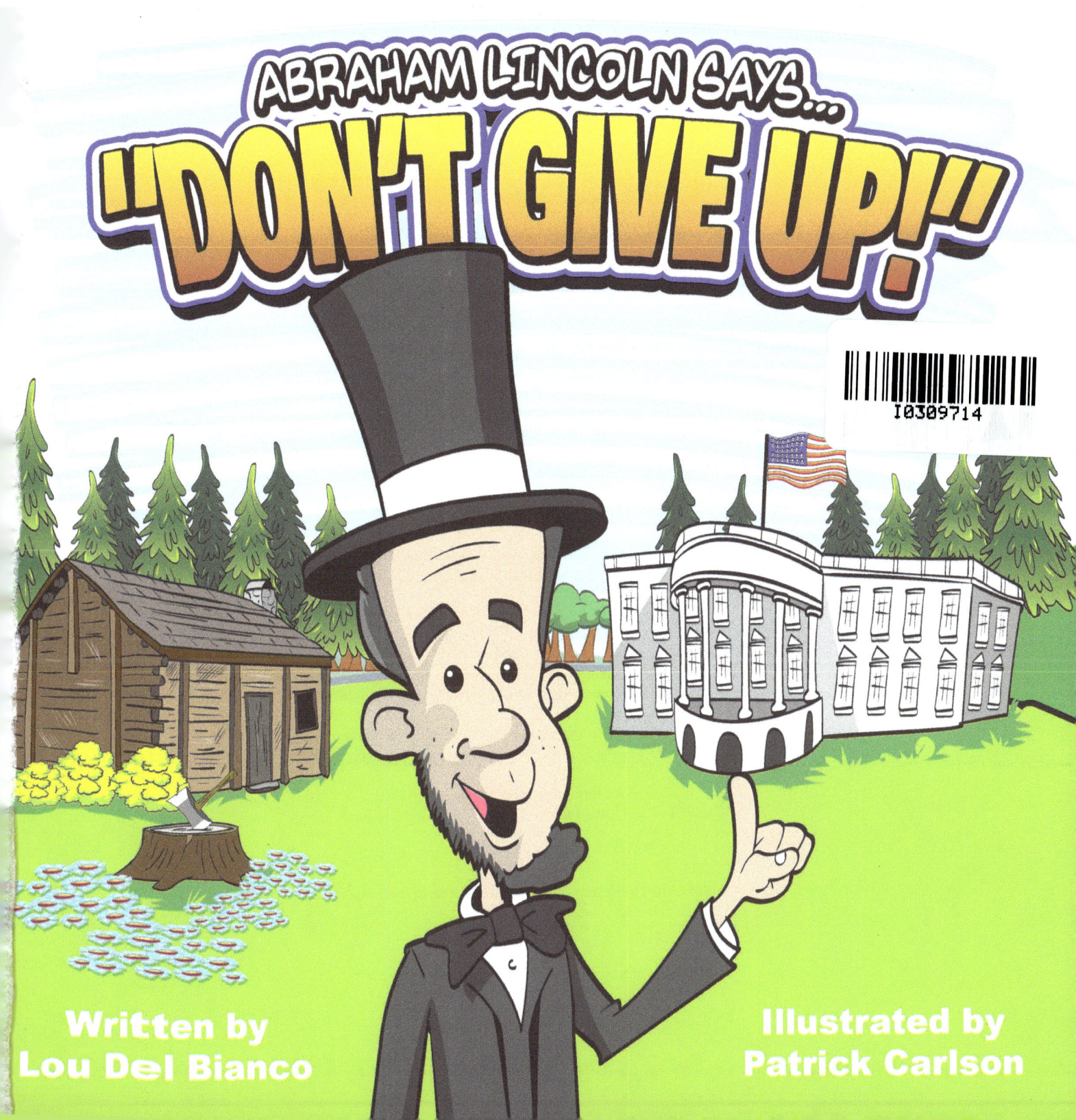

This book is dedicated to:

Anthony Fasano—
for inspiring me to write about my hero.

Camille Linen—
for always guiding me through the creative process
and supporting everything I do.

Text copyright ©2018 by Lou Del Bianco
Illustration copyright ©2018 Patrick Carlson

Published 2018 by Niche Content Press Corporation

All rights reserved.
No part of this publication shall be reproduced or transmitted in any form or by any means, electronic or mechanical, including photocopy, recording, or any information storage and retrieval system, without permission in writing from the publisher.

For information about special discounts and for bulk purchases,
please contact Niche Content Press at NicheContentPress.com.

For more information about booking an event,
contact Lou Del Bianco at 914-937-0897 or lou@findlou.com.

www.findlou.com

Summary: Abraham Lincoln shares his life story and tells how he never gave up while pursuing of his dreams.

ISBN: 978-0-9989987-6-3

Production Design by James Woosley, FreeAgentPress.com

WE HAD NO MONEY TO BUY A PEN,
SO I PLUCKED A TURKEY FEATHER, THEN

I LOOKED AND LOOKED MOST EVERYWHERE,
THEN FOUND THE NEST AND PLACED THEM THERE.
I COULDN'T SLEEP UNTIL I FOUND
THE HOME WHERE THEY'D BE SAFE AND SOUND.

BUT MY LONG LEGS WERE LONG, YOU SEE,
MUCH LONGER THAN SHE THOUGHT THEY'D BE.
SHE SEWED UNTIL HER HANDS WERE ACHIN',
I CHOPPED UNTIL MY ARMS WERE SHAKIN'.

ONE DAY WHEN I WAS CHOPPING WOOD, MY SISTER TILDA THOUGHT SHE WOULD JUMP ON MY BACK AND YELL "SURPRISE!" HER LAUGHTER QUICKLY TURNED TO CRIES.

THAT AX HAD CUT HER ANKLE QUICK,
THE BLOOD FLOWED SO IT MADE ME SICK.
MY SISTER'S SCREAMS FILLED ME WITH DREAD
BUT I REACHED OUT MY HANDS AND SAID:

DON'T GIVE UP!

I MADE A PROMISE STANDING THERE
THAT NEGRO CHILDREN EVERYWHERE,
WOULD ALL BE FREE TO LIVE A LIFE
FREE FROM BONDAGE, FREE FROM STRIFE.

www.ingramcontent.com/pod-product-compliance
Lightning Source LLC
Chambersburg PA
CBHW061147010526
44118CB00026B/2894